GREAT WAR LITERATURE

STUDY GUIDE

Written by W Lawrance

on

STRANGE MEETING

BY SUSAN HILL

Great War Literature Study Guide on Strange Meeting by Susan Hill
Written by W Lawrance

Published by:
Great War Literature Publishing LLP
Darrington Lodge, Springfield Road, Camberley, Surrey GU15 1AB Great Britain
Web site: www.greatwarliterature.co.uk
E-Mail: editor@greatwarliterature.co.uk

First Published as an e-Book 2004
Revised and published in Paperback 2005
Reprinted in Paperback 2006, 2007
Revised second edition as an e-Book 2005

Produced in Great Britain

ISBN 9781905378210 (1905378211) Paperback Edition

Design and production by Great War Literature Publishing LLP
Typeset in Gill Sans and Trajan Pro

Great War Literature Study Guide on

Strange Meeting

CONTENTS

PREFACE

Great War Literature Study Guides' primary purpose is to provide in-depth analysis of First World War literature for GCSE and A-Level students.

There are plenty of other study guides available and while these make every effort to help with the analysis of war literature, they do so from a more general overview perspective.

Great War Literature Publishing have taken the positive decision to produce a more detailed and in-depth interpretation of selected works for students. We also actively promote the publication of our works in an electronic format via the Internet to give the broadest possible access.

Our publications can be used in isolation or in collaboration with other study guides. It is our aim to provide assistance with your understanding of First World War literature, not to provide the answers to specific questions. This approach provides the resources that allow the student the freedom to reach their own conclusions and express an independent viewpoint.

Great War Literature Study Guides can include elements such as biographical detail, historical significance, character assessment, synopsis of text, and analysis of poetry and themes.

The structure of Great War Literature Study Guides allows the reader to delve into a required section easily without the need to read from beginning to end. This is especially true of our e-Books.

The Great War Literature Study Guides have been thoroughly researched and are the result of over 20 years of experience of studying this particular genre.

Studying literature is not about being right or wrong, it is entirely a matter of opinion. The secret to success is developing the ability to form these opinions and to deliver them succinctly and reinforce them with quotes and clear references from the text.

Great War Literature Study Guides help to extend your knowledge of First World War literature and offer clear definitions and guidance to enhance your studying. Our clear and simple layouts make the guides easy to access and understand.

STRANGE MEETING
BY SUSAN HILL

INTRODUCTION

Strange Meeting is a beautiful and moving book. It tells the story of two young men, from very different backgrounds, who, on the surface, have little in common. They meet in the most difficult circumstances, in the trenches of the Western Front, yet manage to rise above their surroundings and form a deep and lasting friendship. It is not so much the war, as the development of their relationship, which forms the basis for this book.

Upon reading this novel, one becomes absorbed into the lives of these men. One shares their feelings and fears, their desperation to survive and enjoy the remainder of their lives. The sights, sounds and even smells which they witness, are evocatively and descriptively brought to life.

This is a story of war and its effects; it is also a story of love, both conventional and 'forbidden'; of human relationships of every variety. This novel shows how, despite the most hideous losses, it is always possible to become a better, more fulfilled person, and above all, to hope for the future.

Strange Meeting demonstrates man's capacity for love, tolerance and caring, despite, or sometimes because of, his surroundings. It is a story told during the worst of times, about the best of men.

SYNOPSIS

This synopsis is divided, like the book, into three parts. It is, quite literally, a summary of the story. It is not, however, intended that reading this synopsis should replace reading the book as here you will only find a list of the main events and in order to get a genuine feeling of the atmosphere created, students must read the novel.

PART ONE

It is the summer of 1916. John Hilliard is on convalescent leave, having been wounded during the Battle of the Somme. He is staying at his parents' house. One night, being unable to sleep he remembers his stay in hospital when he was injured: the sights and sounds of the men around him and his meeting again with a childhood enemy, named Crawford, who is now a doctor. Hilliard is resentful of Crawford's non-combatant status, even though he knows this is unreasonable - after all, someone must tend to the wounded and dying.

Hilliard does not want to sleep. He tries to stay awake and thinks about his homecoming. He feels he does not belong here any more. He knows that he has changed and that everything in England has remained the same.

Eventually he sleeps and the dreams begin - at first they are relatively happy. He dreams of his sister Beth; he misses the relationship they used to share. Then there are the nightmares: he has visions of piles of corpses. When he wakes, he feels sick. He remembers that tomorrow he will return to France and he feels more settled and happy. He wants to go back.

Although it is still dark, he rises and goes for a walk on the beach. He thinks about how out of touch the people at home are with the reality of the war. His parents, sister and even the Major (a family friend) are full of complacency about the war. They have no idea of what is really happening in France. He thinks he can hear the thudding of the guns. Then he recalls childhood events with Beth - memories of calmer and happier days, when she had protected him.

He returns to the house and wakes Beth, believing that he wants to explain his feelings to her - unburden himself and tell her what the war is *really* like. Unsure of himself, he hesitates and Beth takes the opportunity to tell him that she is going to marry a lawyer named Henry Partington - a man twice her age, widowed, with one son. Although he is initially confused by her choice, John soon comes to understand that Beth is taking the only option available to her if she wants to marry and leave home. He also knows now that Beth is lost to him forever and that there is nothing left for him at home.

Hilliard prepares to leave and reluctantly agrees to allow his mother to accompany him to the railway station. Constance Hilliard comments on the poor condition of the platform, stating that Kemble, the stationmaster, has allowed standards to deteriorate. She slips into the conversation, almost as an afterthought, that Kemble's son was killed at Mons. John cannot understand her misplaced priorities and this reinforces the sense that he no longer belongs at home. Constance tells John that his departure reminds her of when he used to leave for boarding school, and that she copes with his absence by not allowing herself to worry. The train departs and John is finally able to relax.

In London, he does some shopping; he has promised to take various items back to France for some of the other men. He buys himself a new cane which makes him feel conspicuously like an inexperienced soldier and he wants to tell people that he *knows* - he's been there and seen the reality of war. He goes to Victoria Station three hours early, still feeling remote and cut-off from everything around him. Suddenly, without explanation, he feels more relaxed and at peace - he can stop worrying and return to the simplicity of life in the trenches: following and giving orders; making decisions; nobody questioning his every move: he is happy - he is going "home".

On the boat, he sleeps - and, for once, he doesn't dream.. When he alights from the train in France, he is met, not by his batman Bates, whom he had been expecting, but by a man named Coulter. Bates, it would seem, has been killed. Coulter gathers together the reinforcements who have also arrived on the train and they begin the walk to the rest camp where Hilliard's battalion are billeted. Coulter tells Hilliard that, during his absence, they have suffered high casualties and that he will struggle to find a familiar face.

Upon reaching his billet, Hilliard is angry to discover that he must share both Coulter and his accommodation with another subaltern - Second Lieutenant David Barton. He had been looking forward to being alone again.

He does not get to meet this new officer immediately as he must report to the Commanding Officer, Colonel Garrett. Hilliard finds that Garrett has changed - he is now complaining, fidgety and agitated. He is no longer the calm and unflustered man that Hilliard remembers. Garrett tells Hilliard of the horrors he has missed - he paints a picture of confusion, a battle gone horribly wrong; delayed orders; faulty equipment; men being shot and blown up; men being mown down by their own guns; no relief. He also tells the story of a man named Clifford, who went mad and shot himself. Hilliard is worried now: can Garrett be relied upon? He seems to have lost his nerve and Hilliard notices that he is drinking heavily.

Upon returning to his billet, Hilliard finds David Barton waiting for him. Barton seems a likeable man, but Hilliard still feels uneasy, particularly about David's ability to confide. Barton amuses the officers over dinner and gradually Hilliard realises that Barton has a quality that he finds it difficult to understand - but he knows, with remarkable suddenness and clarity, that he *needs* Barton's company.

After dinner, the two officers go for a walk. Barton talks openly about himself and his family. This is something which Hilliard has always considered impossible - it would mean revealing too much of himself. But he now realises that he can talk to Barton; in fact he discovers that he has been waiting for someone with whom to share his thoughts. His anxiety fades and he feels more at peace.

When they return to their billet, Barton asks Hilliard how he came to be injured. Hilliard explains to Barton what happened, then retires to bed. Memories of the hospital come flashing back to him. He remembers the man in the next bed and how he had been unable to offer any help, even though all this man wanted was someone to talk to. This remembrance heightens Hilliard's sense of emotional inadequacy and makes him realise that he wants to protect Barton and keep him safe; partly because he knows that the young subaltern has more to offer to himself and the men then he could even begin to be capable of.

Barton writes very long detailed letters to his family, full of jokes and fond remembrances. Hilliards' letters home are a complete contrast - being reserved and polite. Barton's relations start sending messages to Hilliard in their letters and he is gradually introduced to a close and loving family for the first time.

Captain Franklin suggests that Barton should be sent on a gas course. Garrett asks Hilliard's opinion and despite the fact that it would mean a week of safety for Barton behind the lines, Hilliard doesn't want him to go and someone else is sent instead. Hilliard wants to keep Barton nearby - to *know* that he's safe.

Orders come for the battalion to move up to the front lines. After they have finished their work, Barton and Hilliard walk down to the nearby orchard. They come across the burning wreck of a German aeroplane, containing a dead pilot. This is Barton's first experience of death in the war and Hilliard has an overwhelming desire to protect him. Barton, however, is more realistic. He knows that for him, as for everyone, the awfulness has to start somewhere.

PART TWO

During the march to the front, Barton and Hilliard are separated - Hilliard must ride while Barton walks. Barton thinks of Hilliard's detached family, comparing them with his own; and also of their first meeting when he had instinctively known that he and Hilliard would be friends. As they enter their destination town of Feuvry, Hilliard rides by and sees Barton's face. He witnesses a look of shock on the face of his new friend. Just like the demolished town before them, Barton's innocence is being destroyed.

Barton writes letters home and we learn that he feels that Hilliard is trying to protect him from the realities around him by not telling him what it will really be like when they get to the front. We also discover that Barton is disturbed by the noise of the guns and the damage they have inflicted on the surrounding landscape.

That night, in their billet, a sergeant asks if the two lieutenants can help him with a man called Harris who has shut himself in a cellar and is refusing to come out. Initially, as the more experienced officer, Hilliard takes control but then realises that Barton is better suited to the task: his innocence of what is to come and his open and friendly manner will make it easier for him to talk to the young soldier. Barton persuades Harris to come out of the cellar and takes him upstairs, leaving him on a landing while he goes to get his flask - he believes a little brandy will help the man sleep. A shell hits the house and Harris is killed. Barton is wracked with guilt and Hilliard, grateful that Barton himself survived, tells him that this is what the war is like. He suggests that Barton write to Harris's family - believing that this may help him to come to terms with what has happened.

Hilliard notices that Barton has changed: he looks shocked, miserable and exhausted. Hilliard tells him how afraid he had been that Barton himself had been killed in the blast. He also reveals that he needs Barton.

There is a change in Barton's letters as well. He writes of his indifference at seeing unburied bodies; his tiredness; his feelings of hopelessness. Writing like this appears to help and as he writes, he becomes less depressed and more like his old self again.

Two weeks are spent in the support trenches and Barton becomes fidgety; he is beginning to yearn for excitement. Hilliard merely feels settled and contented - at home. Barton and he have become very easy in each other's company. They are relaxed and contented. Encouraged by Barton, his family send letters directly to Hilliard whose desire for Barton's survival has become overwhelming.

Barton is ordered up to the front line to make a map and bring back information. He is pleased and proud to be given this assignment but Hilliard, on the other hand, is full of dread and foreboding that Barton won't survive. Hilliard recognises that his feelings for Barton have deepened and grown into love. Despite the serious implications of this thought, the admission of his feelings, even if only to himself, makes him feel more calm. But then, panic sets in again - what will he do if Barton is killed?

Garrett sends for Hilliard to discuss moving up to the front line.

They discuss Barton, who has already left on his mission. Garrett shows his perception when he points out that Barton has qualities which the rest of them lack and he also shows that he understands the fact that they *all* need him. Hilliard experiences a sense of pride that the Commanding Officer appreciates and values Barton's qualities.

Meanwhile, Barton is making his way through the trenches to the observation post with his guide - a runner named Grosse, when a shell lands just ahead of him. He rounds a corner to find a terrifying scene of mutilation. A little further on a private is shot by a sniper and dies right in front of Barton. Suddenly he is overwhelmed by the pointlessness and futility of the war: he has been sent out here to draw a map, while all around him young men are dying and his map won't help them or anyone else. In a moment of calm, detached insanity, Barton stands up, with his head above the parapet until Grosse angrily drags him back down to safety again.

Hilliard notices that Barton has altered again as soon as he returns. Gone are his openness and warmth and in their place are apathy and silence. Barton won't discuss his assignment - in fact he barely talks at all and Hilliard feels isolated and helpless. Their orders are changed, and they find themselves back behind the lines again.

Barton writes. This time, however, it is not a letter. Instead he is copying passages from his reading book. Later, Hilliard discovers what Barton has written: Is it easier to live or to die, and does that depend on the quality of the life you are left with? Despite reading Barton's notes, Hilliard still cannot understand what he is thinking. Barton seems to neither know nor care what he is doing and Hilliard feels he has failed the younger man. They go to Battalion Headquarters to receive their orders and Hilliard feels jealous of the fact the Barton can still talk and laugh with the other officers and yet remains aloof with him. They discover they are to go back to the front the next day.

That night, Hilliard wakes to hear a tearing sound. Barton has ripped his book and his notes to shreds. He explains that he had been trying to make sense of everything around him but has decided that this is impossible because nothing makes sense. Hilliard is relieved - at least Barton is talking to him now. Barton pours out his feelings - his anger at the deaths he has witnessed and the futility of the war. He also speaks about his feeling of numbness and he is worried that he has stopped being able to feel or care about anything. Hilliard reassures him: the fact that he is able to talk about it means he *does* care; he shouldn't be surprised or ashamed at the feelings he is now experiencing. The two men are eventually able to relax with each other again. Barton tells Hilliard that he loves him.

PART THREE

This opens with a letter from Barton to his family. He tells them, quite frankly and openly about the day-to-day horrors of trench life: rats, lice, wet, death and also of the changes the war has made to him personally.

Hilliard receives a very formal letter from Beth telling him that she is shortly to marry Henry Partington. Barton is stunned by the abrupt tone of Beth's letter. That night, Hilliard and Barton are ordered to gather together a party of men and carry out a reconnaissance of the enemy trenches. They come under heavy fire and are forced back to their own trench. Three men are dead, including Coulter, whom they have been forced to abandon in No Man's Land due to his appalling injuries. When they get back to their own trench, Hilliard is initially angry with Barton because he

(Barton) went too close to the enemy lines and gave away their position. However, when Captain Franklin questions Hilliard about the success of the raid, Hilliard plays down the incident and does not mention Barton's error. Later, he tries to reassure Barton that, even if it was his fault, it was an easy mistake to make being as it was his first time in No Man's Land, and that he should not blame himself.

Barton writes home that he is haunted by what has happened - particularly leaving Coulter in No Man's Land: he's worried that Coulter isn't really dead and believes that there is a possibility that he wasn't that badly wounded after all. He is also shocked by some of his own behaviour: he remembers that he risked his life to save a hedgehog and yet had not attempted to save Coulter.

Hilliard and Barton are ordered, along with the other officers, to attend a meeting with Garrett who tells them that, as he has refused to order any further reconnaissance raids, which he deems unnecessary and pointless, he has been relieved of his command and ordered back to England.

By now it is the end of November 1916. Garrett is replaced by Colonel Keene who is soft-spoken and apparently hesitant, but has a reputation for thoroughness. The men are ordered into battle and despite everything he has already been through, Hilliard knows that this will be Barton's first real taste of war.

The night before the attack, Barton and Hilliard discuss the future; they plan to spend Christmas together with Barton's family. They talk about what lies ahead for them. Barton reveals how afraid he is of what will happen during the battle and Hilliard tries to reassure him that this feeling will pass. Just before they sleep, they speak about their love for one another and how special their feelings are.

Next morning, Barton is no longer afraid, but Hilliard feels a strong sense of foreboding about his friend. The barrage begins at eight o'clock. Eventually they go over the top but Barton and Hilliard are separated. They come under heavy enemy fire and Hilliard soon realises that the attack is hopeless - the men are being mown down by gunfire. It is chaos. Hilliard meets Parkin - a young soldier to whom Barton had spoken the previous night - and they seek shelter in a shell-hole. Hilliard realises that his leg is injured and Parkin offers to go for help. Hilliard, alone in the shell-hole, drifts in and out of consciousness. He dreams of Barton and Beth. In his more lucid moments, he hears the cries of other wounded men. He decides that he must get back to the trench, because he needs to know what has happened to Barton. He drags himself out of the shell-hole towards his own trench, picking his way between the bodies, one of which is Parkin, who had gone barely a few yards before being killed.

By the middle of the next morning, he arrives back at his own lines, but he's at the wrong end of the trench and the men here are strangers to him. They send for stretcher-bearers and he is taken away, despite his desperate attempts to get news of Barton.

When Hilliard wakes, he is in hospital, and Captain Franklin is with him. Hilliard is confused: he doesn't understand where he has been or where he is. His left leg has been amputated but he is, initially, unaware of this. He receives a letter from David's mother which he is afraid to open, but eventually he must. It tells him that David has been reported as missing, believed killed. David's mother begs John to give her any information he has. She writes in loving, warm language of her concern for John. A second letter reveals that David's belongings have been forwarded to his family by Captain Franklin.

Hilliard writes back, telling them that David is almost certainly dead.

He wants them to know the truth - because this is what David would have wanted. He promises to visit them when he is well enough.

Hilliard is sent to a convalescent home where he is visited by his mother. He asks her to get him copies of the books which David had been reading. His only thoughts are of David: he feels remote from everything else - even the loss of his own leg. David's family write and tell him they are looking forward to his visit and are finalising plans. They are full of concern for his wellbeing.

When Hilliard is sufficiently recovered, he visits David's home. Everything is exactly as David had described it. So vivid were David's descriptions, that Hilliard feels as though he has been here before. Once again, and finally, he has come home.

CHARACTER ANALYSIS

This section contains an analysis of the main characters in the novel, concentrating, obviously, on John Hilliard and David Barton. Here, we look not only at how the characters start the book, but the changes which their personalities undergo, as a result of their experiences.

JOHN HILLIARD

John Hilliard is a Second Lieutenant in his early twenties, who, at the beginning of the story, is about to return to his battalion after five weeks sick leave. He had received a leg injury while fighting on the Somme. He feels uncomfortable while he is at his parents' house and cannot wait to get back to the front - which feels more like home to him.

As a young child Hilliard was very insecure and greatly relied on his sister Beth, often sleeping under her bed and, as this was forbidden, creeping back to his own room in the early hours of the morning. His upbringing was typically upper-class and Victorian - staid and devoid of outward emotion. He, therefore, finds it difficult to communicate with others, and is unsure how to respond to those around him, finding conversation awkward. He is reserved and prefers his own company to being among crowds of people.

His meeting with Barton completely transforms his personality. Suddenly, he finds that he is able to talk about himself and listen to others, especially Barton. He looks at those around him differently now: he shows more tolerance, but he is also jealous of any attention which David pays to them. He finds, probably for the first time in his life, that he is able to love someone and to admit that love, not only to the recipient of his affections, but also to himself. Barton has taught him that he is worthy of receiving love too - something of which his life had always been devoid. Now that he has discovered his own capacity for love, he feels that he must preserve this feeling and its object.

It is not so much his war experiences which have affected Hilliard - in fact, at times, he seems almost immune to his surroundings. Instead, it is his friendship with Barton and his new-found sense of love and caring which cause the greatest changes to his personality. During the course of the novel, Hilliard becomes more open, expressive and emotional, although the relationship between himself and his family remains restrained.

He is terrified of losing Barton and he appreciates that war makes all relationships temporary. In losing David, he believes, he would be alone again. The fear of this loss comes to dominate many of his thoughts and actions.

In the end, of course, Hilliard is forced to face his worst fears. It is the love of Barton's family which enables him to cope with his losses. By the end of the story, he has become more optimistic, and prepared to look ahead - even without David, he is a brighter and more positive person.

DAVID BARTON

David Barton is three years younger than John Hilliard and has just arrived in France for the first time. When we first meet him he is lively, with a warm and friendly personality. Barton is an optimist, always prepared to see the best in people, he has a talent for making others feel at ease and they instinctively like him, without necessarily knowing why. He is mature and wise for his years and those around him know that he brings relief to their chaotic world. In short, they *need* him.

One of six children, Barton comes from a very close family. When he lived at home, his father, who is a doctor, had always encouraged David and his siblings to talk openly about their feelings: something which some of his new colleagues, especially Hilliard, find disarming. His letters home demonstrate this. They are very frank and give vivid descriptions of trench life, his experiences and his feelings. Barton's letters contrast with Hilliard's correspondence which is cool and aloof, with little detail and no emotion.

As he gains more experience of the horrors of the war, Barton's personality begins to change. He becomes angry at the waste of life; he is unusually quiet, seeming to care less about those around him, and withdraws into himself. It is not that he is afraid of dying; on the contrary, his worst fear is what his life will be like after the war: if he survives physically, but his personality remains changed, how will he manage? He has grown used to liking people and being optimistic and is confused about the changes he is undergoing. Coulter's death, for which Barton feels chiefly responsible, causes a marked alteration in his character. He becomes even more introverted and thoughtful, yet quite reckless with regard to his own safety.

By the end of the book, with Hilliard's help and love, he has regained some of his old composure; he's more calm and able to talk again; he helps those around him come to terms with their fears, by admitting his own; once again he is putting everyone else at ease. He is excited about "going over the top" for the first time, even though he now has a better understanding of how frightful it will be.

David doesn't survive, but we are left with the impression that those whose lives he has touched are better, more fulfilled, people for having known him.

BETH HILLIARD

Beth is John's older sister and represents the innocence of youth and the life he has left behind - the time before the war, when she was his only friend and looked after him. At the beginning of the story, John is still quite dependant on Beth, wanting to confide in her. In fact, at this stage, he probably looks upon Beth as more of a 'mother-figure' than his real mother. As events progress, however, he comes to realise that he now lives in a world which Beth cannot even begin to understand.

She seems to be a somewhat lost character, confused and less sure of herself than Hilliard remembers her. Many women during the war felt similarly: they could only sit at home, waiting and worrying, and wonder what the future held for them.

Beth has chosen, therefore, to marry: not for love - love is not important to her, when compared with security and the safe knowledge that her husband is still alive. Being twice her age, Henry Partington cannot be called-up to fight, so she will never have to face losing him. He has a son of his own, and this gives Beth someone else to look after, since John has left.

CONSTANCE HILLIARD

Constance Hilliard is John's mother. She is beautiful, poised, tall, elegant, and completely incapable of showing affection. Appearances matter to Constance - the family must always do whatever is required to create the right impression. So, for example, John must visit the Major and discuss the war while home on leave, regardless of whether this is what John wants to do.

The war does not seem to affect her, but even if it did, of course, she would never show it. Her dislike for allowing personal feelings to interfere with duty is demonstrated when she comments on the poor appearance of the railway station, only mentioning in passing that the station-master's son has been killed in action. She seems disappointed that he has allowed his standards to slip, yet makes no allowance for his grief. She does not show any sympathy towards the man either.

Constance cannot outwardly sympathise with John, even when he has been injured and eventually maimed. She does not discuss his injuries with him or what his future holds. She shows concern for John's wellbeing, but in a practical rather than maternal sense: is he being well looked-after; does he want anything brought from home? She comes from a generation, and, to a certain extent, a class which does not readily show emotions and, regardless of John's loss, this is a tradition she intends to maintain.

COULTER

Coulter is a batman (an officer's orderly) to both Hilliard and Barton. He is a happy, self-sufficient, pleasant man with a passionate belief in the justification of the war. He is enthusiastic about almost everything - from his everyday chores to fighting. His belief in the righteousness of the Allied cause, and the innate wickedness of the Germans makes Barton feel uncomfortable.

He also has a 'fey' quality: an ability to know when something is wrong or about to happen. He is popular with both of the main characters and his death has a profound affect on Barton, who feels responsible for leaving him in No Man's Land.

COLONEL GARRETT

Colonel Garrett, who trained as a lawyer, has a wife and four daughters living on the south coast. Hilliard remembers that even before Hilliard's injuries, Garrett had always seemed out of place in the trenches - resembling a city lawyer more than a serving officer. He is not an imaginative man, but is brave, steady, and considerate towards his men.

However, when Hilliard returns from his sick leave and we meet Garrett for the first time, it becomes clear that he has undergone a complete change of personality. He has become an old man: his face is different; his cheeks are drawn in and his eyes are puffy. However, the changes in him are not just physical. Emotionally he seems to be shattered: it becomes clear that the Battle of the Somme and what he witnessed then has altered Garrett beyond recognition. The only similarity between this Garrett and the one Hilliard used to know is his attitude towards his men. His air of calm has disappeared and in addition to this, he now drinks heavily. He has, essentially, lost his nerve.

He begins to doubt his own capacity to lead, asking Hilliard's opinion of decisions. He seeks reassurance from junior officers that he is doing the right thing. Eventually, events overtake him and Garrett refuses to issue any further orders which he feels will needlessly sacrifice the lives of his men. At this point he is relieved of his command. Whether Garrett has taken this action as a means of escape, knowing that he will be sent home, or whether he harbours a genuine concern for the well-being of his men is unclear. His character certainly seems to have been broken to a point where he is incapable of making decisions, although he must realise that this action is not going to end the suffering of his men, merely that he will no longer be there to witness it, or have to feel responsible for their deaths.

CAPTAIN FRANKLIN

Franklin is the Adjutant of the battalion. An adjutant is a staff officer who helps a commanding officer with administrative affairs. He is a tall, efficient, detached man who is very self-controlled and calm in battle situations. He never becomes personally or emotionally attached to the men around him. He also wants to prevent Barton and Hilliard from becoming too close - something for which Hilliard dislikes him. Franklin probably takes this course because he understands the consequences of the death of one of them. He realises such an event will affect the survivor's ability to function properly as a soldier and that functionality is what concerns Franklin the most.

In the end, however, we see a more compassionate side to Franklin. He visits Hilliard in hospital, trying to ensure that the young lieutenant has everything he needs. We also learn that he has written a compassionate letter to David's parents. This demonstrates that, despite appearances, his actions have always been dictated by his desire that the battalion should function at its best; not that he is an uncaring or unfeeling person.

.

THEMES

LOVE AND RELATIONSHIPS

The author herself states that she is often asked whether Barton and Hilliard were homosexual, and whether their relationship was a physical one. She says that it was not her intention that the reader should conclude that the relationship *was* physical, although this supposition would not really change anything that occurred between the two men.

Barton and Hilliard find comfort in each other's company in an otherwise harsh and unfriendly environment; they enjoy sharing the few pleasures that they are afforded - music, books, conversation, companionship and letters home; they illustrate the depth of feeling which can grow between two people, regardless of their circumstances. Whether or not Barton and Hilliard share a physical relationship is irrelevant to the story. It is their deep and profound sense of need, love and compassion which is paramount.

Martin Taylor's poetry anthology *Lads*, deals entirely with the topic of love between the soldiers of the First World War, and explores the nature of these relationships which were not necessarily physical but were, on the other hand, much more deep and meaningful than mere comradeship.

This type of involvement, whilst not necessarily commonplace, was not all that unusual. Some men did have homosexual relationships during the War, either because they were homosexual anyway, or because they simply needed some form of sexual gratification. For many, however, these friendships, formed during almost unimaginable times of fear and personal hardship, were the kind of close and powerful connections which last a lifetime - and are usually more satisfying and fulfilling than a sexual relationship anyway.

A commonality of experiences enabled these men to share a deep understanding, which was not possible with those at home, whose understanding of their troubled emotions and experiences was limited.

Whatever form Barton and Hilliard's relationship may take, it is most definitely the strongest, and most powerful feeling that either of them have ever experienced. Hilliard is amazed at how easy it has been to fall in love, since this is an emotion which has previously been absent from his life. This is especially difficult for him, considering that theirs would have been a "forbidden" love: he can appreciate that there will possibly be difficult consequences to their love, or more particularly, to its discovery, but he does not care.

Another form which these male relationships often took was that of hero-worship - usually inspired in the young by an older or more experienced officer. The soldiers were living in a loveless world, with an understandable desire to prove that people could still care.

Family relationships are also explored. In *Strange Meeting*, Barton has a close and loving family to whom he can talk and write freely and they reciprocate. Many soldiers were keen to keep the harsh realities of trench life from their families, wanting to protect them. A notable exception to this was Wilfred Owen who could always write very openly to his mother about his feelings and experiences. Again, his ability to manage this sometimes shocked others, for example Siegfried Sassoon, who doubted whether Owen's mother would *really* want to know the truth.

Hilliard, on the contrary, has a very formal relationship with his family. Even Beth, to whom he used to feel close, has grown away from him. The letters sent by John's family are emotionless, like their relationship. It is this lack of emotion in his own family that draws Hilliard towards Barton.

CHANGE - NOTHING LASTS FOREVER

Throughout the story, the main characters are constantly changing as a result of the circumstances around them and how they are affected by the events they are witnessing.

In reality, many people were altered by the war, either physically, or emotionally. For some it was the loss of a limb, or a loved one; for others it was the psychological scars which remained. Some recovered fairly quickly, but for many the war remained a haunting experience which would stay with them forever and affect every aspect of their lives.

The two main characters, who are obviously the focus of the story, change drastically; but for entirely different reasons. Barton, who initially is lively, open and carefree becomes cynical and angry. This was a common reaction amongst soldiers in the First World War. Siegfried Sassoon, for example initially wrote patriotic verse, in support of what he felt was a just cause. As he gained experience and discovered the realities of the war, his poetry changed - as did he. He became more bitter at the waste of human life and resentful at the complacency which he felt was being shown by those at home. In *Strange Meeting*, Barton worries that the changes in his personality will be permanent: that if he survives, he will not be the same man he was before the war. Hilliard, who feels responsible for Barton's welfare, is keen to point out that this is highly unlikely. He refuses to believe that someone so capable of giving so much love and affection could ever change to that extent.

Hilliard, on the other hand, alters from an introspective, quiet and insecure man to become a more emotionally sound, caring and outgoing person. He is able to help Barton overcome his fears. This is probably Hilliard's first experience of being emotionally useful to anybody. However, it is Barton who has given him this ability, not the war. It is his meeting and falling in love with Barton which has had the greatest affect on his life. As a child, he was protected by his sister, Beth. Now he feels that he is the protector - he *must* keep Barton safe. This is not just because he is the older and more experienced officer but also because his need for Barton is a greater and stronger emotion than he has ever experienced before, and not one that he is willing to relinquish.

Colonel Garrett's personality also undergoes many changes as a result of having to order so many men to their deaths and experiencing the consequences of his actions. He had started the war as a man renowned for his cool head and bravery, but he has been deeply affected by what he witnessed on the first day of the Battle of the Somme and eventually he becomes unable to continue in his position.

These changes to the men at the front are juxtaposed with the lack of change in the life of those at home. This is typified by Constance Hilliard, whose life seems to remain entirely unaltered despite the events which happen to her son.

MAN'S INHUMANITY... AND HUMANITY

How will a man react when placed in inhumane circumstances? Some will rise to the occasion, as though it were created just for them to prove their mettle; others will shy away, effectively being in denial of their situation. Such reactions, it would seem, are as varied as the men themselves.

Colonel Garrett, for example, effectively shuts down after witnessing the carnage of the first day of the Battle of the Somme. He becomes unable to function properly or to carry out his duties. His is a very "human" reaction. He is revolted at the waste of life, but also at the total chaos and disorder; he cannot bring himself to comprehend that most of the lives lost, were needlessly lost -

either through lack of communication or equipment failure. He feels responsible for the fate of these men and is eventually relieved of his command.

On the other hand, Garrett's second in command, Captain Franklin reacts well under fire. He has never allowed himself to become too closely involved with the men around him, and he is obviously a very private man - in fact, we learn nothing about his home life at all. It is this very detachment which enables him to survive emotionally. His detachment is necessary, however, since it enables him to perform better and allows him a good overall view of how the men are performing - without emotions getting in the way.

One could also examine a man's capacity to help another soldier, regardless of the personal cost. For example, Parkin risks, and ultimately gives, his life to help Hilliard. As we later learn, he barely manages to go more than a few yards before he is killed. This episode demonstrates not only the futile waste of life that the First World War became, but also that to many men, like Parkin, it was second nature to help another man. It would not even have crossed his mind to leave Hilliard there to die alone. This is reminiscent of a poem entitled *Comrades: An Episode* by Robert Nichols, which describes the attempts of an officer, named Gates, who has been wounded and left in No Man's Land, to return to his men in their trench before he dies. Back in the trench, however, at least one of his men is contemplating risking his own life to rescue Gates. He is only prevented from doing so by the arrival of another officer. The impression given in both of these circumstances is that the men regarded it as an honour to help their officer

FATE AND FATALITY

"Seize the day" or "live for the moment" were fairly common sentiments amongst the soldiers of the First World War, especially if they had personally survived a close-shave with death, or witnessed the killing of someone nearby. Many decided that as they were going to die anyway, they might as well do so with their heads held high, enjoying themselves. There are many stories of men carrying out outrageous acts, which could be said to be reckless. Sometimes, these acts are carried out without thinking - such as when Barton stands up in the trench. He does this, almost to prove a point; namely that his life is of no more value than any other man's.

Upon first reading Strange Meeting, it becomes clear that, inevitably, one of the main characters is destined not to survive; that despite, or maybe because of, the powerful and ardent love between Hilliard and Barton, there will be no happy ending for them. Fate has thrown them together in the worst possible circumstances and they have managed to rise above their environment and discover a serene, detached world of love and contentment. That this should not be allowed to continue to the end of the story, and the two men should not be allowed to explore their new-found love in less difficult surroundings, demonstrates that war has the most inhuman of consequences. This also makes the reader ask the question: would their love have survived? If both men had lived and had returned home, would their feelings have retained the same intensity, or were those feelings the result of their situation? The threat of imminent death, would naturally make their emotions very raw and profound, but that does not necessarily mean they would not have outlived those circumstances and developed further at the end of the war.

The positive outlook at the very end of the book, where Hilliard is now looking forward to the future, whatever it may hold, leaves the reader with the sensation that love is stronger than war; that whatever has happened in the past or might happen in the future, he has become a better and stronger person, not through war, but through love.

COMPARISONS

This section of the Study Guide compares some of the themes in *Strange Meeting* with those in *Journey's End* by R C Sherriff, *Regeneration* by Pat Barker and *Birdsong* by Sebastian Faulks as well as various works of poetry.

The first important point to note is the time of publication. *Journey's End* was first published in 1929, while *Strange Meeting*, *Regeneration* and *Birdsong* were all published in the second half of the twentieth century (1971, 1991 and 1993 respectively). R C Sherriff had served in the trenches and wrote from first-hand experience, whereas Susan Hill, Pat Barker and Sebastian Faulks have based their works on extensive research. These factors all make a difference to both the content and style of the books.

Within these four books, one of the main themes explored is relationships and the effects of war upon them. The two main characters in *Strange Meeting*, Barton and Hilliard, fall deeply in love. As has been stated previously, their love was not necessarily physical, but that does not make it any less intense or meaningful - if anything, the opposite is true. Hilliard comes from a background devoid of affection and, finding this in Barton and his family, he is able, for the first time in his life, to experience real love. There is not really an element of hero-worship between Barton and Hilliard, more a sense of mutual respect and admiration, as well as a feeling of being comfortable in each other's company.

In *Birdsong*, the relationship between Stephen Wraysford and Michael Weir bears some scrutiny. Wraysford is very clearly heterosexual while Weir appears to be ambivalent towards women because he has no experience of relationships with them. The relationship between these two men is very different from the one between Barton and Hilliard. During the course of the novel, Weir comes to depend heavily on Wraysford, looking up to him and treating him, almost, like a good-luck charm. Wraysford, on the other hand, finds it difficult to become emotionally attached to anyone and it is not until Weir's death that he really appreciates his own feelings of friendship towards his lost comrade.

In *Journey's End* the main relationship explored is that between Stanhope and Raleigh. Stanhope is the senior officer and Raleigh is the new recruit, determined to do well. Unlike Barton and Hilliard, these two men knew each other before the war and, in fact, Stanhope has "an understanding" with Raleigh's sister. They attended the same school and, Stanhope being good at sport, became an object of hero-worship to Raleigh, even before the war. This is really the limit of their relationship. Raleigh looks up to his friend, while Stanhope wants to protect the younger man - as he has always done. Stanhope's reactions to Raleigh are also tempered by his fear that Raleigh will inform his family, and therefore his sister, of the effect that the war has had on Stanhope. The impression created is that Stanhope has always been popular with Raleigh's family and he is terrified of losing their respect. He has, in fact, managed to avoid seeing either his or Raleigh's family for some time - he would prefer them to remember him how he was and he can deal with his responsibilities more efficiently, knowing that they continue to believe in him. There is no hint of homosexual love between these two men.

Within this theme, one could also study the relationship between Siegfried Sassoon and Wilfred Owen as portrayed in *Regeneration*. Owen hero-worships Sassoon - after all he is a courageous officer, renowned for his daring exploits at the front, and of course, a published poet - something of which Owen, at that stage, can only dream. Like Raleigh, Owen is always prepared to excuse any sign of rudeness or bad behaviour in his hero, and his feelings within the relationship are by far the stronger. Like Stanhope in *Journey's End*, Sassoon is the more experienced - not only officer, but poet. He wants to guide Owen's poetry and assist him with its publication. Again, though, there is no obvious symptom of romantic love displayed between Owen and Sassoon, although Sassoon begins to doubt this, based on the content and style of Owen's subsequent letters.

One could also look at a poem by Sassoon entitled *The Last Meeting* which was written following the death of David Thomas, a young handsome officer, for whom Sassoon had developed a deep emotional attachment. This beautiful poem tells of the inspirational qualities which David had and how his death will have repercussions throughout Sassoon's life.

In *Birdsong*, *Regeneration*, and in *Strange Meeting*, the author is able to hint at homosexual elements. This was not a freedom which R C Sherriff would have been able to enjoy. It is unlikely that his play would have been performed had the content been overtly homosexual. In 1929, people were still keen to ensure that the love that had existed between men during the war was comradeship, rather than anything physical.

The effect of the war on these relationships varies. In *Strange Meeting*, without the war, there may not have been a relationship in the first place. Barton and Hilliard meet at the front and the whole of their time together is spent there. For them, there is no home life, no leave and very little separation. They know that they might die at any moment and this serves to intensify their feelings for one another. The sense of impending loss and danger adds to the fear and risk necessarily involved in such a close friendship between two officers at this time.

In *Regeneration*, Sassoon and Owen also meet as a direct result of the war, but in completely different circumstances to Barton and

Hilliard. There is not the same sense of fear involved in their relationship, other than the fear which Sassoon has associated with the discovery of his sexuality. This is partly due to the different nature of their friendship, and the fact that the effect of the war is confined mainly to their future prospects and poetry. Throughout most of the novel, we cannot be completely sure that either man will ever return to the front, so their outlook is different from that of the characters in Strange Meeting who face imminent death almost every day.

In Journey's End, the relationship is different again. Stanhope and Raleigh, had a pre-existing friendship, so the entrance of the war into their lives changes their relationship. Gone are the days of school cricket and rugby. Stanhope, who has been serving for many years, has become war-weary; his personality has changed, almost beyond recognition; his outlook has become tempered by his experiences. Through Raleigh we experience this loss of innocence and are able to compare this with Stanhope's pre-war personality.

The effect of the war on the individual is also worth noting here. Not only in the case of Stanhope's changed personality, but also we can observe in Strange Meeting, the alteration in Barton and Garrett, both of whom exhibit changes of character due to events they have witnessed. On the other hand, Hilliard in Strange Meeting and Wraysford in Birdsong have been altered not by the war, but by love. In Hilliard's case, it is his love for Barton and its reciprocation that have brought about his changed personality. Wraysford, on the other hand, has been so deeply wounded by his broken relationship with Isabelle, that nothing, not even the war, seems to really touch him now.

Another aspect of the war, which these books examine is that of responsibility - looking after the men. In Regeneration, Sassoon's stated reason for wanting to return to the front is to be with his men. He has an acute sense of guilt that he is safe, while they are dying in France. Robert Graves points out that this feeling is mutual. This is a subject which, in reality, Sassoon felt strongly about. Once he had decided to return to the front, he wrote a poem entitled *Banishment*, in which he tries to explain his reasons for making his 'Declaration', shows how his attempts to end the war have failed and asks his men to forgive him for abandoning them. This is a moving poem which demonstrates his sense of responsibility and affection towards his men.

In *Strange Meeting*, however, Hilliard's main concern is the welfare of Barton. That is not to say that he doesn't care about his men, but he knows that Barton is better suited and more able to meet *their* needs. He feels that, for everybody's sake, but especially his own, Barton must survive.

Throughout *Journey's End* it is clear that Stanhope always puts his men first. He regards himself as their father-figure, although in many cases he is much younger than them. He knows and accepts that it is his responsibility to ensure that his men are performing at their best, both for their own benefit and for the good of the company. Like Barton, in *Strange Meeting*, he is quite prepared to discuss his own fears in order to ease those of his men.

In *Birdsong*, Wraysford, who is emotionally quite a challenging character, eventually acknowledges his faith and affection for his men. He states that he would entrust his life to them. This is not a characteristic which he had granted even to Isabelle, whom he has finally confessed to be the love of his life. It seems that the bond with his men and the trust he places in them, is stronger than the conventional love he feels for Isabelle.

Finally, we can look at the subject of loss. In *Regeneration* Wilfred Owen is so bewildered at the prospect of leaving Sassoon that he finds this sense of loss unquantifiable; many of the patients of

Craiglockhart are there because they have been unable to cope, mentally, with the losses they have had to experience. Some of them have been permanently wounded, not physically, but psychologically and must learn to come to terms with these feelings. This is a central theme in *Regeneration* - the journey from initial loss to survival - the rebuilding of men.

In *Journey's End*, Osborne's death is treated differently by the two main characters. Raleigh feels guilty that he survived while Osborne is still lying out in No-Man's Land. Stanhope, who has lost his best friend, reacts differently. He appears not to care - he appears to carry on as though nothing has happened. This is because he knows that to think about it will stop him functioning. He must continue to perform his duties because his men are relying on him. Stanhope is not given the opportunity to dwell on Raleigh's death as he is called upon to meet his own fate. Although it is not clear, the impression given is that Stanhope also dies.

Wraysford, in *Birdsong* has a much harsher character, but when he is buried underground with Jack Firebrace, he comes to better appreciate his fellow man. His reaction to Jack's death is, however, anger and disappointment, rather than grief. He believes that Jack has given in, and chosen the easier option of death, rather than fighting for his life. Of course, Jack has already faced great losses himself, with the death of his young son and many of his friends, so his admission of defeat in the face of his own death is quite understandable.

Strange Meeting is, by far, the most hopeful of these books and yet the surviving character has arguably the most losses to contend with. Not only has his beloved Barton been killed but his own leg has been amputated. Barton's death has always been his worst fear - he has always been unsure, having discovered love and his own capacity for it, that he could carry on without the object of that love. Due to this, he feels that the loss of his leg is of secondary importance. His own, emotionally starved, family hardly know how to react to him, but Barton's family pour out their affection. Through this he is able to face the future and even his great fear of being alone is pushed aside in favour of optimism for the future. Despite his loss and grief, Hilliard has learned new qualities of caring and tolerance: emotions born of love.

FURTHER READING

Wilfred Owen: The Truth Untold

by Dominic Hibberd

A definitive biography of Wilfred Owen, which looks at Owen the poet as well as the man. This is a refreshingly realistic book which includes an open discussion of Owen's sexual tendencies.

The Complete Memoirs of George Sherston

by Siegfried Sassoon

An autobiographical account of Sassoon's life before and during the First World War. Sassoon has changed the names of the characters and George Sherston (Sassoon) is not a poet. This trilogy (made up of *Memoirs of a Fox Hunting Man*, *Memoirs of an Infantry Officer* and *Sherston's Progress*) demonstrates the effects of the war on both the serving soldiers and those left at home.

For a list of the fictional characters and their factual counterparts, see Appendix II of *Siegfried Sassoon by John Stuart Roberts*.

Letters from a Lost Generation: First World War Letters of Vera Brittain and Four Friends

by Vera Brittain, Alan Bishop (Editor) and Mark Bostridge (Editor)

A remarkable insight into the changes which the First World War caused to a particular set of individuals. In this instance, Vera Brittain lost four important people in her life (two close friends, her fiancé and her brother). The agony this evoked is demonstrated through letters sent between these five characters, which went on to form the basis of Vera Brittain's autobiography *Testament of Youth*.

Not About Heroes
by Stephen MacDonald

Probably one of the most underrated First World War plays, this details the meeting between Wilfred Owen and Siegfried Sassoon. It is a humourous, tragic and above all, moving account of this friendship and is based on diary entries and extracts from autobiographies.

These books and others may be purchased through our Web site bookstore at: www.greatwarliterature.co.uk/bookstore.html

BIBLIOGRAPHY

Lads
by Martin Taylor

Minds at War – The Poetry and Experience of the First World War
Edited by David Roberts

Birdsong
by Sebastian Faulks

Regeneration
by Pat Barker

Journey's End
by R C Sherriff

Siegfried Sassoon - the War Poems
Edited by Rupert Hart-Davis

OTHER GREAT WAR LITERATURE STUDY GUIDE TITLES

Paperback Books

All Quiet on the Western Front	ISBN 9781905378302
Birdsong	ISBN 9781905378234
Journey's End GCSE Study Guide	ISBN 9781905378371
Journey's End A-Level Study Guide	ISBN 9781905378401
Regeneration A-Level Study Guide	ISBN 9781905378395
The Return of the Soldier	ISBN 9781905378357
Female Poets of the First World War - Vol. I	ISBN 9781905378258
War Poets of the First World War - Vol. I	ISBN 9781905378241

Great War Literature Study Guide E-Books (Electronic Books) on:

Novels & Plays

All Quiet on the Western Front

Birdsong

Journey's End GCSE Study Guide

Journey's End A-Level Study Guide

Regeneration A-Level Study Guide

Strange Meeting

The Return of the Soldier

Poets

Harold Begbie

Rupert Brooke

Female War Poets I

Female War Poets 2

Female War Poets 3

Wilfrid Wilson Gibson

Julian Grenfell

E A Mackintosh

John McCrae

Robert Nichols

Wilfred Owen

Jessie Pope

Isaac Rosenberg

Siegfried Sassoon

Charles Hamilton Sorley

Edward Thomas

Robert Ernest Vernède

Arthur Graeme West

Please note that e-books are only available direct from our Web site at: www.greatwarliterature.co.uk and cannot be purchased through bookshops.